WHERE'S PJ?

by

Bil Keane

FAWCETT GOLD MEDAL • NEW YORK

WHERE'S PJ?

© 1974, 1975 The Register & Tribune Syndicate, Inc.
© 1978 CBS Publications, The Consumer Publishing
Division of CBS Inc.

ALL RIGHTS RESERVED

A Fawcett Gold Medal Book published by arrangement
with The Register & Tribune Syndicate, Inc.

ISBN 0-449-13982-4

Printed in the United States of America

10   9   8   7   6   5   4   3   2   1

"PJ! You're awfully quiet! Is everything all right?"

"When you see a dot on the ceiling that wasn't there before, then that's a fly."

"He has your eyes."

"There are 22 pieces of bread in a loaf. Did you know that, Mommy?"

"Here, Kittycat! Here, girl!"

"Tell us some of the cute things we used to say,
Mommy."

"Are any of these sandwiches with no covers peanut butter and jelly?"

"It's my mommy's sool-wet . . . sill-et . . . it's her
SHADOW!"

"We'll play cards with you, Daddy, but you'll have
to keep score 'cause we don't know
all our numbers."

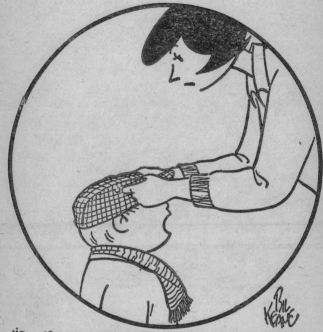

"But, if you put my earflaps down, I won't be able to hear when you call me."

°"Mommy, did you tell Daddy he hadda take a nap?"

"We'll be right there as soon as we see the end of
this commercial."

"Daddy's boss of the backyard and the basement —
Mommy's boss of the kitchen, the living room,
the bathrooms, the bedrooms . . ."

"There's no snow, so why do I have to wear a snowsuit?"

"Am I slow or fast?"

"Only two more numbers to go and Grandma will be here."

"If Santa doesn't have the kind of bake set I want,
tell him to go to Bunn's Toy Store — they
have it."

"That means we're wishing EVERYBODY a Merry
Christmas — even the man across the street
who told us to get lost on Halloween."

"Was Santa's beard BLACK when you were little, Grandma?"

"Kittycat's getting 'cited about Christmas 'cause she
likes to get into the boxes and play with
the wrappings."

"Look here! Cookies? Dolly! Jeffy! PJ! Come get a
cookie! Look!"

"Have you been a good boy?"
"Haven't you been watching?"

"Can Santa speak EVERY language in the world?"

"Aw — when you said Daddy was bringing home a
point-setter, I thought it was a DOG."

"Shall I tell God what I want for Christmas, too?"

"MERRY CHRISTMAS, EVERYBODY!"

"We should've asked Santa for some SNOW, too."

" ... and, oh yes, Aunt Nancy? Mommy says to
thank you for whatever it was you sent
me for Christmas."

". . . and we'd like you to sit for us on New Year's Eve."

"Your price is HOW MUCH?"

"Daddy said 'Happy New Year,' but I don't think he meant it!"

"If you're bad you'll get whiskers, too."

"Daddy, are you gonna be joggin' near a store that sells batteries?"

"How do you like our snow person?"

"Mommy, will you itch my back?"

"I looked in the medical book and THIS is what a
heart's s'posed to look like."

"He's retired. That means he graduated from work."

"Daddy, how old were you when you were my age?"

"Do I put 'Ms.' or 'Mrs.' on Grandma's letter?"

"But they look too NEW to wear! Can't I just wear
'em around the house 'til they look old?"

"If I didn't go to Mark's party could I just stay home and play with his present?"

"Ouch! Daddys don't make very good mothers."

"It's okay if he bites you, mister — he's had his rabies shot."

"This is Mark. He's my fifth best friend."

"Can you open the door for me, Mommy? I've got a
whole crowd in my arms."

"You went outside the lines when you colored that squirrel."
"That's why I like elephants better."

"Is it going to be Saturday all day today?"

"I didn't study for any eye test, did you?"

"You'll **hear** a lot **more** goin' on if you'll put that
thing on my tummy."

"Mommy says 'no' and Daddy says 'yes', Grandma.
Will you break the tie?"

"This is my WRITE hand 'cause I write with it."

"I kissed Daddy goodnight and his whiskers BIT me."

"The reason Mommy is our mother is 'cause she
BORNED us."

"Mommy, are you asleep or just pretendin'?"

"When your boss is out sick do they send a substitute?"

"Boy! Do I have HARD homework for you tonight, Mommy!"

"Don't you think 'The Birdie With A Yellow Bill' has just about had it?"

"I like Granddad's idea better. He put a SHIP in a bottle."

"If you're not good the barber will use this strap on you."

"I don't wanna save for a rainy day. When it's rainin' Mommy won't let me go out to buy anything."

"What kind of a while will we get there in — a little or a long?"

"This looked like more fun on the television commercial."

"She's playin' dishes."

"How come that arrow doesn't have any feathers?"

"If you want me to read to you you'll have to stop
turning pages looking for pictures."

"I think Kittycat's fingernails need trimming."

"Here's a very 'portant paper you're supposed to fill
out for school, Mommy."

"Can I go with you sometime to see the rat race, Daddy?"

"You're Romeo and I'm Gillette."

"What's in this box marked 'frmmps and klums'?"

"Daddy's right! Inflation is really bad. Bubble gum's
TWO cents now!"

"Can we have Chicken Little soup for lunch?"

"Why didn't her grandmother live in a retirement community like all the other grandmothers?"

"Lift me up to the ceiling again, Daddy? You did them THREE times and you only did me TWICE."

"A short distance call for Daddy. It's Mr. Ferrell next door."

"PJ's ball rolled under your bed, but I got it for him."

"Look, Mommy! Here comes the bride!"

"The water's hot, Mommy! I can see its breath!"

"I AM doin' my homework. It's to bring in rags for art."

"I'm in here emptying pockets."

"This ruler's been lost for a long time, but I finally found it — in my desk drawer."

"Mr. Lincoln is runnin' away from home!"

"Aw, come on, Daddy! Make yourself light!"

"I said I didn't need any help!"

"Billy's really my friend, but since he isn't .home I'll come in and play with his little brother."

"Mommy, is it okay if we get wet?"

"Do WE get presents for Father's Day?"

"It's a list of places where people we know used to live."

"You're enough to try the patience of a saint!"
"Mommy, was there ever a Saint Mommy?"

"You better get down out of Mommy's shoes before you fall and get hurt!"

"Do you have to be good at spelling to be a fireman?"

"I'm not the oldest in the family--Daddy is."

"Shall I run home and ask Mommy to jog up here
in the car to get us?"

"Robert Hagan's brother is REAL old! He's
'bout 20!"

"'Cause you only put mayonnaise on ONE side of the bologna and I like it on BOTH sides."

"Danny's mother is 'specting a baby but we have to wait till November to find out if Danny's gonna be a big BROTHER or a big SISTER."

"What did I tell you about bouncing balls against the house?"

"Mommy, which station has that Happy Christmas music on it?"

"I'm tired of Billy bein' the oldest. Why couldn't God have done ME first?"

"I think this scribble spells a word! Now I won't have to PRINT any more!"

"Does everybody have grandmothers? Even poor people?"

"I fell asleep when you got to the part about the
middle-sized bear sayin' 'Who's been sitting
in my chair?' What happens next?"

"I win. Jeffy almost made one basket, but I almost made two."

"Oh, boy! There's my magnet . . . and my good ol'
racer . . . and my best marble, and . . ."

"Mommy! Jeffy's not in his bed!"

"That's three o'clocks of bananas."

"I can't learn to write very good — I wish they'd teach us TYPING instead."

"Oh boy! This is the place where we eat with our hands!"

"Mommy, will you tell Billy to stop breathin' so loud?"

"I was just blowin' on the spoon 'cause this soup is too hot."

"No fair! I just got up for a minute and Kittycat took my seat!"

"I'm so lonesome — somebody kiss me."

"The stick is so you can take it out of your mouth if you want to talk."

"You better not spin my brother around too much 'cause he gets chair sick."

"Can I sleep with you, Mommy? I'm scared 'cause the
TOOTH FAIRY was in my room!"

"That's a potato bug, Jeffy."
"You mean he'll grow up to be a potato?"

"David's mother is taking yogurt lessons. It teaches
you to lie on the floor and stretch."

"Grandma is very smart. She can knit, talk and watch TV all at the same time."

"But, Mom! I have to rest up for the football game this afternoon."

"I'm gonna get all my friends to autograph my bandage."

"Daddy said the days are startin' to get longer, but ours ends at the same time as always."

"You trapped my finger in the knot!"

"A pronoun is for when you don't know the noun's name."

"My balloon popped and scared my ears!"

"Stop wiggling or you'll have a ghost!"

HAVE FUN WITH THE
FAMILY CIRCUS

LOOK WHO'S HERE!	M3419	95¢
PEACE, MOMMY, PEACE	M3417	95¢
PEEKABOO! I LOVE YOU!	M3418	95¢
WANNA BE SMILED AT?	M3332	95¢
WHEN'S LATER, DADDY?	M3411	95¢
MINE	M3370	95¢
SMILE!	M3517	95¢
JEFFY'S LOOKIN' AT ME!	1-3688-4	95¢
FOR THIS I WENT TO COLLEGE?	1-3829-1	95¢
CAN I HAVE A COOKIE?	M3375	95¢
THE FAMILY CIRCUS	M3374	95¢
HELLO, GRANDMA?	M3401	95¢
I CAN'T UNTIE MY SHOES!	M3310	95¢
I NEED A HUG	M3402	95¢
QUIET! MOMMY'S ASLEEP!	1-3930-1	$1.25
WHERE'S PJ?	1-3982-1	$1.25